SEVEN STRATEGIES
THAT SET THE TOP 1% OF
BUSINESS OWNERS APART

**A 15-Minute Guide to Protecting Your Revenue
and Making Partnerships to Strengthen Your Business**

Table of Contents

Three Biggest Threats 1

Strategy One 2

Strategy Two 5

Strategy Three 8

Strategy Four 10

Strategy Five 13

Strategy Six 16

Strategy Seven 18

Why We Wrote This Book 22

Author Bios 23

What are the three biggest threats to your online business right now?

The digital age has changed how most of us do business, and keeping up with new improvements and innovations is critical to success. After a few decades doing business in the digital marketing realm, we've learned a few tricks of the trade, and this guide will share them with you.

Our book focuses on three main threats to your online revenue and ways to approach them when planning for the next twelve months:

1. *Marketplace sites like Amazon drive down margins and enable increased competition from manufacturers and suppliers.*
2. *Larger sites and big box stores drive up paid search costs and benefit from recent algorithm changes on search engines, making it harder to get quality traffic.*
3. *Internal marketing staff, SEO, and pay-per-click agencies are struggling to keep up with an evolving marketplace and maintain high ROI levels.*

To spell it out, you're facing rising client acquisition costs, working harder and harder each year, and making sure all your "expert" resources really do all they can to help you. Does that sound familiar?

What can be done to fix this cycle? Over the past seven years, we have tracked the performance of thousands of small and medium e-commerce businesses and interviewed the CEO's of the top performing 1% to find out what they do to set themselves apart. Here are the top seven strategies you can implement in your own business.

Strategy Number One: Identify Your Weak Points

We've worked with hundreds of CEOs, so we understand that everyone has their own opinion on the benefits of outsourcing versus internal staffing. Most business owners make an effort to hire employees to complete certain work "in-house," especially in areas they consider a core part of their business model. This logic is generally fair, because having full-time employees give you more control and oversight of their work. This approach also allows you to retain accumulated knowledge and intellectual properties should an employee be terminated or leave their position.

If you operate a business that depends on the Internet for a large portion of its leads and revenue, it's easy to extend this same logic to online marketing initiatives. Depending on the size of your organization and the amount of revenue your online efforts generate, you may have a single person or a small team managing your website, social media channels, and email marketing campaigns. However, while large companies can often sustain a completely in-house marketing staff, for a majority of businesses, this isn't the smartest solution.

There are three main reasons successful companies outsource to compete digitally. Outsourcing allows

1. *Rapid platform evolution, ensuring your business is aware of best practices for any site, app, or platform at all times.*
2. *Accelerated training requirements, which keeps the people completing your digital marketing tasks at the top of their game.*
3. *The use of specialized software that can be difficult to learn and even more difficult to use.*

Rapid Platform Evolution

While it will vary from industry to industry, there will always be a myriad of standard platforms you'll need to promote your business. Even the most common ones, like Facebook, LinkedIn, and Google, require a deft hand to utilize effectively. Best practices for these platforms and others constantly change and become increasingly complex. They require more time and effort for employees to stay up-to-date with changing requirements and regulations. Lack of awareness or a failure to engage on any critical platform can spell death for your business, which makes outsourcing an attractive option.

Accelerated Training Requirements

Because platforms change at such a rapid pace, the training employees need to keep their skills current also evolves regularly. Training on a new platform requires a serious time investment, and most employees simply do not have the bandwidth to complete training requirements and do the work assigned to them. These trainings can also be incredibly expensive. Professional marketing firms often financially support this kind of training for their own employees, but smaller businesses don't have the time or budget. Again, outsourcing covers these costs and time investments for you, which means when a contracted employee shows up to work, they already know how to do their job.

The Use of Specialized Software

As the number of platforms and marketing channels companies use continues to grow, the need to monitor brand assets, coordinate content, and optimize ad buying across those channels also grows in importance. Many agencies have created or invested in specially-designed software to make these processes simpler, or pay hefty licensing fees to have a popular system do it for them. While these tools give organizations a leg-up over their less sophisticated competitors, lots of smaller businesses can afford to use them, making outsourcing resources a more affordable choice.

What Should You Do?

These dynamics drive surges of outsourcing, especially when it comes to tech-based services. While it may be appealing to have full-time employees managing some of these duties, it is necessary to complete a realistic assessment of their skills and available work hours. If you stretch employees too thin—either because they don't have the ability or the time to complete their assigned tasks—looking to outside partners may be the way to go.

Power Questions for Employees

- What tasks take up the most energy and time each week? Could outsourcing some of the important or technical-driven tasks help you accomplish more revenue-driven work?
- What tasks do you feel qualified to handle? What tasks would benefit from outsourcing expertise?

Power Questions for Outsourcing Agencies & Contractors

- What software or systems would you use to accomplish my most important tasks?
- How do you ensure you or your employees stay current when systems, programs, or algorithms change?

Strategy Number Two: Focus on ROI - Not Cost

As a CEO, you have to work with a lot of different people. Whether it be internal staff, outside contractors, or other business associates, it's easy to get lost in some of the day-to-day. The biggest mistake we regularly see from CEOs is when they focus on budgets or cost over the ultimate ROI.

Successful executives start by asking the right questions that lead to a blueprint for success, as opposed to just a list of things that will be done for a given budget.

Power Questions

- What will it take to increase our sales in this area by X% over the next 12 months?
- Given our business size and position in relation to our competitors, how much do we really need to invest to effectively compete? In areas (SEO, paid search, social, mobile, affiliate, etc.) should we focus our investments?
- Given my product and service set, my current positioning and my budget, what high ROI activities should we focus on?
- How can we ensure that we quickly eliminate non-performing activities and focus our dollars on profitable ones? What metrics should we use to identify these high performing initiatives?
- What is a reasonable expectation for overall ROI for the investments I make?

Playing to Win

Generally people don't get the results they want from their initiatives because they're not asking the right questions. They focus on the budget rather than getting an accurate picture of the needed investment that will lead to a positive ROI. Your company competes directly with other companies that also invest in the same kinds of services you provide. So the need to understand where you need to position your business in relation to them can't be understated.

Many companies fail because they invest too little or try to take on major competitors with too little ammunition. Your trusted advisors will tell you when you're underestimating the task. But watch out for those who will take your money and give you false hope your plan will succeed when it really won't.

If you use outside contractors to assist your business, you also need to calculate the additional costs on your end to support that work the vendor does. You may need to spend additional staff time to augment their efforts and implement recommendations. It's important to factor these costs into your overall budget as well as your ROI calculations so you get a true sense of the return. Think about it like this, "What do I need to invest into a program so that I win? So that I become relevant enough to attract clients and build significant ROI?"

For example, say you want to enter a marathon. You talk to a trainer and say, "I want you to train me for a marathon, but I'm only willing to spend two hours a week for it." A trainer who is desperate for money and doesn't really care will say, "Ok, sure. I'll work with you for whatever time you have. I'll put together a plan and we'll get started next week." But a master trainer who really knows what they're doing will look at you and tell you they won't waste their time on someone who isn't dedicated and likely won't even finish the race.

A Case Study: ROI vs. Initial Spending

A client who runs a professional services firm came to us doing about $1,000,000 in online sales per year. Sales had been flat for a while and they wanted ways to increase revenue. When we spoke to them originally, we talked to them about what they wanted to accomplish. They had worked with a vendor for the past two years and the CEO was adamant that he wasn't willing to increase the budget or invest any further.

We got into a deep conversation with the CEO about his objectives and defined his goals for growth. It became clear he needed a different kind of partner, one that could do more comprehensive work than the company he currently worked with. And doing more work was going to be more expensive. In fact, doing what he wanted to do would almost double the budget he had currently set.

The conversation turned to ROI versus budget. Over the course of our discussions, we realized he could see significant increases in sales by adopting a different strategy with a different partner, but it would require an additional investment. Ultimately, he took our advice and decided to go with the company we recommended. The additional cost was $3,000/month more than what he previously paid. With the new program in place, his sales tripled! We calculated the ROI, which earned this company almost a 900% return, a huge win for this CEO. But he never could have achieved that with his previous fixed budget.

Strategy Number Three: Set Clear Expectations

After hiring and managing thousands of employees and negotiating hundreds of marketing service contracts, we've found two areas that are usually responsible for poor contract relationships: a lack of specific deliverables, and lack of specific communication expectations.

Lack of Specific Deliverables

When outsourcing to an agency or independent contractor, there is generally a defined deliverable you'll expect to receive: a set amount of content to be created, a number of products to manage, a certain increase in ROI, etc. However, while these deliverables may be agreed upon verbally, they must also be defined in a written contract. This is your responsibility as the project manager or company owner. It is imperative that the signed contract you share with your outsourced employees expressly stipulate exactly what you will receive.

Power Questions

- How can I quantify the work you're doing? What specific tasks can I expect to be completed at the end of every month?
- After the first phase of implementation, what kind of timetable will we use? What deliverables will I receive on an ongoing basis?

Lack of Specific Communication Expectations

Planned deliverables will solve some of your problems, but without a communication schedule, even the best-laid plans can quickly fall apart. Determine how often you'll speak with your contracted workers. While "as-needed" communication can often be a go-to for some vendors, push for a stricter communication timeline. With predictable check-in times, be they weekly, bi-weekly, or monthly, you and your contracted workers know what to expect and will be held accountable for important action items.

Power Questions

- Who will be my point of contact during our partnership? How often will we communicate?
- What should my team prepare before a scheduled call or meeting to make them as productive as possible? What information do you need from me in order to be successful?

Strategy Number Four: Focus on the Account Manager When Contracting

Falling in Love with the Salesperson

If you have contracted out different marketing services in the past, then you know some of the worst companies sometimes have the best sales people. They know exactly what to say, and have expert experience selling the big brands and experience of their firm. In the sales process, they talk about the work they've done for brands like Honda, or Nike, or IBM, then supplement that experience with white papers and other collateral.

If you really focus on this aspect of their pitch, you'll probably think, "Wow, these guys must really know their stuff. Honda wouldn't work with just anyone." But the truth is, the best account managers work with these big brands, ones much bigger than yours. These sales people build rapport and confidence with you and convince you that everyone on their team will be just as good.

We're not here to knock legitimate salespeople and the work they do. But a lot of companies in the online marketing space have adopted a business model that specifically focuses their resources on sales at the direct expense of service, because they believe it is cheaper to acquire new clients than it is to retain them. This is the "churn-and-burn" model at its best (or worst). We strongly recommend vetting an actual account manager before signing a contract. Because when it's all said and done, they are the ones you will depend on for results.

The Importance of Account Manager Selection

As part of the build-out of our national network, we have evaluated thousands of companies and hundreds of individual account managers within those companies. We went into online marketing companies and invested the time to understand the account management structure and its impact on performance.

We learned that 99% of the success of your relationship with an online marketing company will be determined by your specific account manager.

Oftentimes when a sales manager closes a new account, it goes into a lottery system for account manager assignment based on which persona has the most availability. Newer, less experienced account managers who don't yet have a full book of clients get a majority of the newly signed clients. We see this especially for small businesses who sign with a large agency.

Account Managers Drive Your Experience and Results

It may seem obvious, but not all account managers are created equal. Our experience tells us that most companies have very little formal or ongoing training. Nor do they have fixed procedures related to the communication cycles and work which account managers put into individual accounts. This results in an extremely high correlation between campaign performance and individual account manager assignments.

After evaluating the performance of hundreds of campaigns, we found account managers who consistently ranked at the top end of the scale not only increased the performance of the campaigns they are over, but also retained their clients longer. They had more frequent communication, better follow-up, and generally happier clients.

So How Do I Get a Good Account Manager?

It's very simple. You need to ask for one! More specifically, tell the vendor that you need to know who your account manager will be before you sign the contract. Talk to your new account manager, interview them, and even look up their professional background. What are their values? What's their skill set and expertise? Ask specific questions about your website and how they plan to help improve it. If you don't like the answers, ask for a different manager from the start.

Power Questions

- What experience do you have with the specific services I'm contracting for?
- What training and certifications do you have?
- Have you worked on similar-sized accounts in the past?
- What is your plan to increase revenue for my business? Why?
- What's the best way for us to communicate regularly?

What If You Think You Have a Bad Account Manager?

Demand to switch. You should do this immediately and without hesitation. Wasting time trying to make a bad account manager into a good one isn't your problem. It's a training issue that the vendor needs to address. You need never be shy about calling the senior manager at a vendor and asking for a new account rep if you're not happy.

Remember, it's absolutely imperative to evaluate the company you're going to contract with. But if you don't evaluate it all the way down to the actual account manager you'll be working with, you risk the performance of the entire campaign. Don't be dazzled by their client list, collateral, or Powerpoint decks. Focus on the people that will actually do the work for you!

Strategy Number Five: Learn to Identify the Bad Apples Fast

Like a lot of business dealings, working with vendors usually requires a bit of gut instinct. But knowing what to look for can make weeding out the bad apples from the good ones even easier. We've found there are three common "red flags" that may indicate an unstable partner relationship: a lack of transparency, a refusal to grant you access to certain accounts, and falsified reporting.

Lack of Transparency

In the simplest of terms, transparency is the ability to show and tell. A company that lacks transparency may refuse to show you completed content, make a detailed list of changes they implemented on your website, or provide you a reference sheet of the links they shared on certain social platforms. If a company refuses to let you see the work they do on your behalf, the work (if you ever do see it) will most likely be subpar.

Access to Accounts

Outsourcing account management may look desirable, but if a contracted firm or employee refuses to allow you access to those accounts, you may be in danger. Companies who engage in this practice will often say they manage a particular account under their own master account or through an internal system. But don't believe them. If you pay for a third party service, you should have access to your account at all times. This isn't just to manage the revenue these projects may be creating; you'll also need the data and intelligence these accounts provide to truly make your business successful in the long run.

Falsified Reporting

In order to track the success of any marketing campaign, a reporting system must be in place. If your contractors refuse to show you any reporting data, this is a warning sign. SEO is usually the most likely place for false reporting, with vendors generating reports that are either overly complicated or outright fabrications.

Every reporting document, regardless of its subject, should be easy enough for you to understand or for the account manager to explain. If you cannot understand the reports, or your account manager cannot break down the details in a way you can understand, there's probably a reason.

A Case Study: Why Asking the Right Questions Matters

At one point, a client we helped came to us and said, "My marketing company is doing a good job, but I'm still not seeing the increase in sales I thought I would." When we asked how he had come to that conclusion, the client showed us a report created by the agency he had hired.

The report showed the client had 65 "conversions" on his paid search campaign from the last month, which the vendor had classified as completed sales from clients who had clicked through on paid ads. However, the client reported that the site had only processed 43 sales in total in the same period. "I just don't know why things aren't adding up," he told us. "I mean, the numbers from Google can't be wrong, can they?"

We called the vendor to do some digging, and began by asking direct questions about the "conversions" tracking they completed. We also asked them about the AdWords account they had started on behalf of our client. It quickly became apparent the agency made several mistakes with the tracking pixels on this particular campaign, and that the real conversion numbers on the client's pay-per-click campaign (PPC) were much lower. They could not explain how the mistakes had occurred or why they had been reporting numbers that weren't correlated to the Google Analytics reports for several months.

Due to these errors, the vendor relationship between the two firms was short-lived, and we quickly found our client a new business partner to accomplish the tasks initially given to the original vendor.

Spotting the Bad Apples

Like any industry, digital marketing has a few bad apples. Unlike other industries, they can be even more difficult to spot. Digital marketing is rife with "churn-and-burn" companies that spend the majority of their time strategizing how to sell, mislead you, and still retain your business with little or no focus on completing actionable deliverables.

Getting on the Right Side

Your long-term business strategy should be based on industry-standard best practices and align with the specific interests of the platforms you use. If you ask the right high-level questions, you will arrive at the right conclusions, and you will find it easier to spot a bad apple from a good one.

Ethical companies will train their employees and contractors to be ethical too. Companies and employees who are dedicated to "white-hat" tactics will consider things like alignment, best practices, and industry guidelines when making decisions and crafting a strategy. They will not use words like "gaming", "tricking", or "masking", and they won't suggest you dedicate time creating junk content or engaging with partnerships whose policies and procedures are not above board. They do not make promises they are unable to keep, and they do not make guarantees about things they cannot control. Avoid the temptation to go for the quickest, easiest solution—if something sounds too good to be true, it usually is.

Power Questions

- How do the strategies your firm uses benefit the end user?
- How do the action items completed by the vendor create a better user experience on both a search engine and our website?

Strategy Number Six: Be Careful Who You Take Advice From

Good Intentions, Bad Advice

As your business strategy evolves over time, you have to be conscious of who you ask for advice. If you work with an outside firm heavily geared toward social media marketing, they're likely to emphasize social media and push you into spending more money and strategizing in that area. The same situation would play out with a pay-per-click company, an SEO company, an affiliate marketing company, etc. Given this fact, it's critical that you seek out input and advice from people who don't have a vested interest in one specific type of service or marketing platform.

It's important for business owners to get some outside opinions about the overall strategy they wish to implement. Just asking vendors how they should approach things won't be enough, partly because those vendors are obviously biased towards the types of services they provide. The advice these vendors offer isn't meant to be spiteful or given in malice. It's honestly because that's what they know. Their industry is what they believe in.

Aside from specific vendor bias, it's also important to be aware of a constantly changing marketplace. In previous chapters in this book, we talked about ROI being the metric that's most important. As you track ROI, you will see certain types of activities drive higher ROI than others as time goes along. When you see these trends emerge, it's often in your best interest to move investment dollars from one type of activity to another. Unfortunately, if it means losing a contract, most vendors won't be eager to highlight that to you.

Search for the Highest ROI Use of Funds

As CEO, your question shouldn't be "Can I make positive ROI on this activity?" Instead, ask this power question: **"Is this activity the highest ROI activity available to me right now?"**

Those are two very different questions. If you ask the latter one, it forces you to look at all services available to you and evaluate the potential returns that you could get. If you ask a vendor or someone specifically involved in one aspect of online marketing, they're very likely to tell you about what they do most often. That solution worked for them. To that person, it will also work for you. But solutions don't work the same for all businesses. It's not a one size fits all. You also need to ask this question broadly in your business and put up against other offline marketing opportunities like print and direct sales.

A Case Study: Investing in the Best ROI Activity for You

We have a client who is an e-commerce specialty products company that came to us spending five figures a month on pay-per-click ads and $3,500 on an SEO company that did content marketing for them. We looked at the overall investment they made each month, how the campaigns performed, and the blended cost of traffic. We recommended they reallocate their content marketing budget into a contract with a new vendor for a special type of technical SEO work. We also suggested they overhaul and restructure their paid search program.

By making those changes, that company was able to increase organic traffic 35% in just 90 days. That created an additional $30,000 per month in sales. So by lowering their blended cost of acquisition overall, they were able to be more competitive with their paid search campaigns. Then they expanded their reach into new ad networks. Altogether their efforts drastically increased ROI for this company.

Getting quality outside advice and perspective on your marketing programs proves worth the effort.

Strategy Number Seven: Learn to Manage Integration

As the owner or manager of a business, you have a responsibility to create an integration system between internal resources and outside vendors. Your success in this endeavor will impact how you leverage the dollars you invest in a digital marketing service. We've identified four best practices to consider when designing an integration system: establishing communication loops, leveraging your resources, creating a team mentality, and sharing vital information.

Establish Communication Loops

There are two communication loops you need to establish with an online marketing partner.

1. *A regular, scheduled call to review reports and discuss upcoming action items, This call should include your internal marketing staff, and they should come prepared with questions to ensure everyone's priorities are in sync.*
2. *Direct, impromptu communication via email and phone between your staff and your vendor account manager, especially when new products or services are launched, changes are implemented to the website, or seasonal specials or events take place.*

The account manager for your organization will most likely have experience working with other clients and experience in your industry that can help them implement best practices with ease. Team members also have varying levels of experience, so simply asking good questions can give you great information.

Power Questions for Your Vendor

- What are some of the best practices for this type of work?
- What practices, ideas, or solutions are working for your other clients? Can you implement some of these for us?
- What trends have you seen emerge in the past few months or years that may be relevant to our business?
- What do you think we can do to increase our number of conversions?
- If you were in our position, what would you do that we are not?

Leverage Your Resources with Your Vendor's Expertise

Although outsourcing work generally means less responsibility for you, it would be foolish to leave your vendor without the ample amount of resources you have at your disposal. Working to absorb best practices and industry knowledge from a contracted firm ensures that your company knows what to do when your contract ends.

Power Questions for Your Vendor

- What can my team do to accelerate your work?
- Where would you recommend we devote our resources if you had access to my team's time?
- How can our team be more involved with our online marketing campaign so our efforts have a higher chance of success?
- What can we do on a weekly and monthly basis to enhance your efforts?

Create a Team Mentality

After finalizing an agreement with a new partner, incorporate them as a full-fledged member of your team as best as you can. Integrate your account manager into communication cycles that include your internal planning meeting, and encourage them to become invested in your long-term success, just like you would with your internal employees. Remember that people work to make money, but they'll work harder for people they like.

Share Vital Information

Vendors needs accurate data to succeed, and if you're able to provide it to them, do. Sharing information breeds trust and common accountability to the goals you share. It also helps protect against a vendor hiding mistakes or shielding data.

Practical Tips for You & Your Staff

- Learn how to read and understand analytic data yourself. Ask detailed questions about your traffic and conversions to help you comprehend it clearly.
- Provide Google certifications to some of your internal team members. This will give your team the ability to understand what vendors do and how they can help them succeed. The certification is not expensive, and can give your team a competitive edge.
- Set up bi-weekly or monthly calls or meetings. Ask your team to come to these events with a summary of their completed action items and questions about how to proceed going forward.

Stay Connected at the Top

This is our final recommendation: talk to the CEO of each of your vendor companies at least once a year. Tell them about your experience with their team and how they're impacting your future revenue goals. Ask them about their thoughts and experiences within your shared industry, and what general trends they're seeing that may affect you. Simply scheduling a call with the CEO will trigger an internal review of your campaigns, a status update from their team, and ensure everyone who has a hand in your company's account with their firm is communicating with the right people. It also gives you much-needed visibility at the top level, and puts you front-of-mind with senior executives, who may have insider introductions or recommendations that could benefit you and your business.

Why We Wrote This Book

As entrepreneurs ourselves, we have a very personal connection to the challenges of a growing business. We've spent years in our own businesses learning the marketing lingo, hiring, firing, making money, losing money, and struggling to keep up with the rapidly changing landscape of online marketing and e-commerce. We have also struggled with when to hire internal staff or outsource to a vendor, and also how to effectively manage contractors and their work.

Driven by our frustrations and learning experiences from these challenges, we helped build the first national quality and performance vetting service for online marketing companies. It started from a simple idea to find the best specialist agencies in the country. We want to help companies get great deals from these agencies, and make sure they perform well on the back-end. Since inception, Grow Team experts have evaluated and thoroughly vetted hundreds of online marketing companies and helped thousands of small and medium-sized businesses contract with them for their services. We are the first true buyer's agency for online marketing services and continue to grow our national presence at a rapid pace.

This book is our way of sharing the knowledge and experience we've gained from negotiating hundreds of online marketing service contracts with a large group of business owners.

People often ask us if giving away our knowledge actually undermines our businesses. The answer is definitely not. By telling people about what we do, and by sharing our experiences, we can help people manage the process for themselves. And we also help to inspire a lot of people to call us and ask us to help them improve their businesses and take advantage of the thousands of hours of work we've already put into researching and negotiating these kinds of contracts. We further our mission of helping business owners become more educated buyers of online marketing services.

Author Bios

David Moses

David Moses is an experienced executive with a history of leadership roles in both early-stage entrepreneurial organizations and established private equity-backed groups.

He has extensive experience building sales programs, increasing online revenue, building brands, and improving operations through a disciplined, metrics-driven approach.

David is passionate about helping other business owners succeed in a rapidly changing environment and he's dedicated to the long term success of our clients.

Originally from New York, David has two amazing daughters and currently resides in San Diego. David has served on several industry boards and was chairman and a board member of the charity Gift for Life.

Max Helmer

Max Helmer is a senior executive with experience in all aspects of early stage company growth. He has an in depth understanding of the online and digital marketing industry as well as SaaS applications.

He has a broad base of experience in negotiating and managing contracts with outside suppliers, focused on generating long term performance and results.

Max was born and raised in San Diego and loves working with small business owners to help them grow their companies.

WANT TO TALK TO US?

We help companies find the best partners at the best price.

If you'd like us to evaluate your business and tell you what we think, just give us a call and tell us that you read our book.

800-741-9298   growteam.com

Made in the USA
Coppell, TX
06 August 2020

32506278R00016